THE MOST
IMPORTANT
DECISION
YOU WILL
EVER MAKE

THE MOST IMPORTANT DECISION

YOU WILL EVER MAKE

Understanding What It Means to Accept Christ

JOYCE MEYER

WARNER
Faith®

NEW YORK   BOSTON   NASHVILLE

Scripture quotations are taken from the
King James Version of the Bible.

Scripture quotations noted AMP are taken from *The Amplified Bible, Old Testament* copyright © 1965, 1987 by Zondervan Corporation. *New Testament* copyright © 1958, 1987 by the Lockman Foundation. Used by permission.

Warner Books Edition
Joyce Meyer Ministries Inc.
P. O. Box 655
Fenton, Missouri 63026
All rights reserved.

Warner Faith

Hachette Book Group USA
1271 Avenue of the Americas, New York, NY 10020
Visit our Web site at www.warnerfaith.com.

Printed in the United States of America
Revised and Updated Edition: October 2005
First Warner Faith Edition: February 2003

10 9 8 7 6 5 4 3

ISBN-13: 978-0-446-69816-0

ISBN-10: 0-446-69816-4 (Special Sales Edition)

Do you need a friend?

Do you need to have your sins forgiven?

Do you need peace?

Do you need a future?

If you answered yes to any of these questions, please keep reading . . .

CONTENTS

I

THE MOST IMPORTANT DECISION YOU WILL EVER MAKE

I would like to talk to you about a very important decision. As a matter of fact, this is the most important decision you will ever face. This decision is more important than where you choose to go to school, your career choice, who you decide to marry, or where you decide to live. This decision concerns eternity. Think about it. Forever is a long, long time.

So many people are concerned only with today or a few months down the road. At best, some are concerned with retirement. I want to go beyond that. I want to talk about life after death. Are you making any provision for that?

Did you know that you are not just a body made of flesh and bones, blood and muscle? You are a spirit being, with a soul, and you live in a body. When you die, which everyone does sooner or later, your physical body will be put in a grave. It will decay and turn to ashes and dust. But what about the *real* you—the inner you, your personality, your mind, will, and emotions?

Think of the spiritual part of you as the part of you that cannot be seen with the natural eye. This part of you will live forever. And where the spiritual you lives depends on the decision you make as you read this book.

There are two forces in the world: good and evil, right and wrong. We know that truth even without being told. There are two forces in the spirit realm: God and the devil; good angels, which are spirit beings God created to help Him carry out His business, and bad angels, called demons.

These bad angels were once good angels who made a choice to rebel against God. Lucifer, an archangel (also called Beelzebub, Satan, or the devil), led these angels in rebellion, and God cast them out of heaven.

God and the good angels have their home in heaven. Satan and the bad angels have their home in hell.

Between heaven and hell is the earth and the atmosphere above the earth. Good and bad angels patrol the earth at all times. Satan also roams about, "seeking whom he may devour." The Bible tells us that in 1 Peter 5:8. The Holy Spirit of God (God's own Spirit) also dwells on the earth as well as in the heavenlies, and the job God has given Him is to seal, keep, preserve, and protect God's people (those who have chosen to serve God). The Holy Spirit also has the job of wooing and winning people who have not yet chosen God and His way of living.

Have you made your choice? The choice is yours. No one can make it for you. God created you with a free will, and He will not force you to choose Him. He did not force the angels to obey. Part of them rebelled, but remember, *bad choices bring their own penalty.*

2

HAVE YOU ACCEPTED CHRIST AS YOUR SAVIOR?

Are you born again (born anew from above)? What does it mean to be born again? What does the Bible say about being born again? In John 3:3 Jesus said,

I assure you, most solemnly I tell you, that unless a person is born again (anew, from above), he cannot ever see (know, be acquainted with, and experience) the kingdom of God. (AMP)

Nicodemus, the man Jesus was speaking to, asked, "How can a man be born when he is old? Can he enter his mother's womb again and be born?" (John 3:4 AMP). Perhaps you are thinking the same thing. How can a person be born who has already been born? Jesus was speaking about a spiritual birth. Earlier I said you are a spirit, with a

4

soul, and you live in a body. Our bodies have already been born, but the Bible teaches that our spirits and souls are dead and dark because of sin.

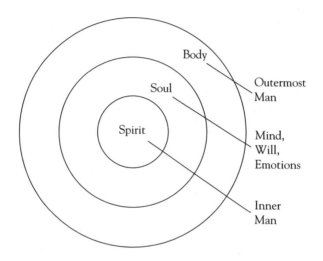

Diagram: The Three Parts of Man

You may go look at yourself in the mirror and move your head, arms, and legs. You are breathing. You can say you are alive. But is the *real* you alive? Are you alive and full of light *inside*? Do you have peace? Are you at peace with yourself? Do you like yourself? Do you have joy and hope? Are you afraid to die? These are all questions you need to ask yourself. *You can put a smile on your face and still not be smiling inside.*

When Jesus spoke of being born again, He was teaching that the inner man must come alive to God. John 3:6 says, "What is born of [from] the flesh is flesh [of the physical is physical]; and what is born of the Spirit is spirit" (AMP).

When mothers give birth to babies, they are flesh born of flesh. When God's Holy Spirit comes into your human spirit, you are then spirit born of Spirit. This is referred to as *the new birth*. The Holy Spirit only comes into your spirit *one way*. You can be born again *only one way*. Just as physical birth can take place only one way, so it is with spiritual birth.

You cannot impart spiritual life to yourself any more than you could cause yourself to be born physically apart from the natural process. A natural physical process has to be in operation for a baby to be created, and a supernatural (spiritual) process must be in operation for your spirit to receive new birth.

What is the process? If you decide today that you want to be born again (accept Jesus Christ as your Savior), what do you need to do?

First, recognize and admit that you are spiritually dead, due to sin in your life. Romans 3:23 says, "For all have sinned, and come short of the glory of God." *No person is without sin!* Don't be afraid to admit you are a sinner. First John 1:8 says:

If we say we have no sin [refusing to admit that we are sinners], we delude and lead ourselves astray, and the Truth [which the Gospel presents] is not in us [does not dwell in our hearts]. (AMP)

Verse 9 says:

If we [freely] admit that we have sinned and confess our sins, He is faithful and just (true to His own nature and promises) and will forgive our sins [dismiss our lawlessness] and [continuously] cleanse us from all unrighteousness [everything not in conformity to His will in purpose, thought, and action]. (AMP)

Beloved, that is *good* news. No wonder the gospel is referred to as *the good news.* So we see *Step 1* toward accepting Christ is to *admit* you are a sinner. That means face the truth about yourself. It is hard to face the truth. It hurts to admit our faults. Satan wants to keep you in deception. God wants you to face the truth.

Step 2 is to *confess* your sins. *Confess* means to speak forth. It has a cleansing effect if you speak forth out of your mouth the things you have done wrong and from which you want to be free. Those things are lodged inside of you, and they are the very things—the memory of those

7

things, the sensing of them being wrong—that have filled you with darkness.

Confess them to your Father in heaven. It is God's way of delivering you from them. You get rid of them by confession, and He replaces the sin with forgiveness. He cleanses you. It is like getting a bath inside.

I was born again (accepted Jesus Christ as my Savior) at age nine, and I vividly remember feeling as if I had just been scrubbed on the inside. I felt clean, light, and fresh inside. Beloved, you can get in the bathtub or shower and give your body a bath. You can scrub your outside clean, but only Jesus can cleanse your inside.

3

Who Is Jesus?

I have mentioned Jesus a few times but have not told you about Him. It is very important that I tell you about Jesus because it is impossible for you to get right with God without knowing Jesus. It is impossible to accept Jesus Christ as your Savior without knowing Him.

I said in the beginning that you have a very important decision to make. Everything about that decision depends on your understanding who Jesus is and what He has done for you. Then your decision is simply whether you believe it and receive it, or you choose to continue in darkness the way you are if you have not accepted Christ as your Savior.

I am about to tell you something that will not make much sense to your head, but your heart will want to believe it. So get ready to hear an amazing true story that can change your life forever.

The Bible says in Genesis 1–2 that in the beginning, God created the first man and called him Adam. God formed his body out of the dust of the ground and breathed into him His own life and Spirit, and Adam became a living soul. In other words, he came alive inside as God breathed into him a portion of His very Self. God's breath was put into the man, and he came alive. He was full of the life of God.

God called him Adam. The Bible says Adam was created in God's image (Gen. 1:27). There were things about Adam that were like God. He had God's breath. He was holy and good like God. There was no evil in Adam at all. He and God could fellowship because Adam was created in God's image.

The Bible says light cannot fellowship with darkness. God and Adam were both light, so they could fellowship together. *Adam was comfortable with God.*

Are you comfortable with God?

Adam was also created with freedom of choice (the opportunity to exercise free will). God told him what was right but gave him the ability to choose. Adam was good, but to stay good, he had to *continually* choose God and God's ways.

God realized Adam needed a helper, a mate. So He put Adam to sleep and took one of his ribs, then He closed up his side (see Gen. 2:21–22). From Adam's side, He made woman to stand beside (be*side*) Adam as a help-mate, a companion. Notice that woman was not taken out of Adam's feet, because he was not to stand on her. She was not taken out of his head to be over him, but she was taken out of his side to be beside him in life as his partner.

Now we have a couple living on earth in a paradise, a beautiful garden God created just for them. It is pretty obvious God wanted them to enjoy life.

Are you enjoying life?

There was another creation on the earth, an unpleasant one, Satan, who had previously fallen from God's original plan for him as the archangel of praise and worship. He fell through rebellion, through wanting more than what God had given him. He wanted to be in control, not under God's leadership.

He said he would exalt his throne above God's, and God threw him and the angels who were in rebellion with him out of heaven. Hell was made for them, but Satan and multitudes of other demon spirits still had access to earth's atmosphere for a time.

There is a time set aside in God's plan for all of them to be eternally confined in hell, but right now, God is still allowing the devil (Satan, Lucifer) access to the earth because men and women are still in the process of *choosing* whom they will serve. In order to have a choice, we must be offered more than one thing.

God offers life, light, joy, faith, peace, righteousness, hope, and all good things. Satan offers death, darkness, despair, depression, devastation, dread, fear, and everything bad.

Even as I write these things, I think, *Why would anyone choose Satan and his ways?* Yet multitudes do. Many people are deceived. They are choosing the wrong way because they lack knowledge. Hosea 4:6 says, "My people are destroyed for lack of knowledge." Perhaps you have not had enough knowledge to make a good choice until now. I am making this truth available with the hope that multiplied thousands make the right choice.

Let's go on with our story. Adam and Eve (as Adam named her) were enjoying life in the garden. God gave them charge of the earth. He told them what they could and could not do; remember, they had freedom of choice. God told them what He wanted them to do, how their lives could be blessed, but did not *force* them to do it.

He had placed a lot of fruit-bearing trees in the garden for them to eat of freely, but the fruit of one tree He told them not to eat: "the tree of the knowledge of good and evil" (Gen. 2:17). You might be wondering why God even put the one tree there and told them they should not eat its fruit. Remember, in order to have choice, there must be more than one selection. If they were going to choose to obey God, they had to have something they could choose to disobey.

God wanted their love and obedience. Obedience is actually a fruit of love. He wanted it, but it meant nothing to God if Adam and Eve did not give it as an act of free will, as a result of their own choosing.

Would you be excited and blessed if others loved you because you forced them to, leaving them no other choice? God created man with freedom to choose, and He left a few very important choices. You are in the same situation today. Your freedom to choose gives you the opportunity to make very important decisions.

To go on with our story, Adam and Eve were enjoying life, enjoying God, the garden, the good fruit, each other, and all the other things God made. Genesis 3 tells us that Satan appeared to Eve in the form of a serpent. She was not afraid of the serpent (snake) as you or I might be today. The serpent was not a bad animal. Satan was using it to appear to her in that form.

Through the serpent, he began to pose questions to Eve that made her wonder (reason; the kind of reasonings that 2 Corinthians 10:4–5 talks about, which sets itself up against the true knowledge of God) why God told them not to eat of the tree of the knowledge of good and evil. Actually, God did not want them ever to know anything about evil. But remember, they had to have a choice.

God had told Adam that if he ate of the tree of the knowledge of good and evil, *he would surely die* (Gen. 2:17). He meant that they would die on the inside, not the outside—not their physical bodies. He meant the life in them would die out. The light would go out, and they would be dark.

Recently a man who had lived a terribly sinful life had surgery. He thought he might die, and he wanted to get right with God. As Dave and I talked to him, he said, "I feel dead inside."

Think about it. He wanted to accept Christ because he was afraid he was going to die (physical death) on the operating table, yet in reality, he had been dead inside all of his life, and he said so with his own mouth.

Are you alive or dead?

The serpent lied to Eve. He said, "You shall not surely die" (Gen. 3:4 AMP). What he said was the *opposite* of what God said; therefore, it was a lie. God's Word is truth. And here in the beginning, you can see the nature of Satan.

He is the exact opposite of everything God is. God wants you to have everything good. Satan wants to destroy you. He accomplishes this through deception today, just as he did with Eve.

He continued to lie and pose questions to her. Eventually she followed the devil's advice and talked her husband into doing the same. They both disobeyed God by eating the fruit He told them to avoid. The result was exactly what God said: They died spiritually.

The next time God came into the garden to visit Adam and Eve, they hid from Him because they were afraid.

Have you been hiding from God because you are afraid?

Hiding did them no good. God knew they had sinned. They had believed Satan's lies. They had fallen into the temptation and were now having the fruit of their choice. Fear is the fruit, or result, of sin.

You may have the fruit of your choice.
But remember, some of it may be bitter in your mouth!

God began to deal with them concerning their sin, but He also had a plan for their redemption and deliverance from the mess they had gotten themselves into. In Genesis 3:15,

15

God told the serpent that the "offspring" (the seed of woman) would bruise his head, and he (Satan) would bruise the heel of the "offspring" (AMP).

He was speaking of Jesus, His only begotten Son, who was already in existence spiritually. God is a triune God. We refer to Him as *the Trinity*—one God in three persons—Father, Son, and Holy Spirit. Each of the holy Persons of the Godhead has a major role in your life.

Jesus already existed spiritually, but in order to help man out of his mess, Jesus would eventually need to come to earth. He would need to get inside a natural human body like yours and mine. He would need to humble and lower Himself to become a human being. Remember, Jesus is all God, the Son of God. In other words, *very God of very God.* He certainly was and is very much God.

God had a plan, but it would not occur until the exact right timing in God's overall plan. Ephesians 3:10 (as based on the wording in *The Amplified Bible*) reveals the purpose of God, which is that through the Church,[1] God's wisdom (His many-faceted and infinite variety of wisdom) might be made known to the principalities and powers that are the demon spirits and their ruler, Satan, who rebelled.

In plain English, we are *in a war—a war between Satan*

and God! It is already established, and always has been, who wins the war. God does. The victory party is planned.

Whose side are you fighting on?

If you are serving Satan and believing his lies, you are working for a loser. God has the winning team.

Anyway, this is ultimately God's plan. He will use His people—people who love, obey, and serve Him willingly—and Satan will be defeated.

You may wonder why God allowed us humans to be in this war. Remember, Satan defeated God's man in the garden and stole from him what God wanted him to have. Actually man, through deception, gave it to the devil.

What God is doing—and has been doing since the garden and will keep doing until the job is done—is this: *He is equipping man with the ability to regain what Satan stole from him.*

Jesus is the key to the whole plan.

Let me continue our story from Genesis 3 where God told the serpent that eventually his head would be crushed (his authority destroyed). God had spoken forth what would happen, and if God says it, eventually it happens.

But before it happened, two thousand years went by while men and women multiplied on the earth. Sin and trouble also multiplied. Where sin flourishes, so does trouble.

Man was unholy, unrighteous, and no longer right with God. The sin principle dwelt in man's flesh. He had a sin nature. In other words, sin was the natural thing for man to do. He did not have to try to sin; he just did. In fact, he could not stop himself.

Every time children are born, they have the nature of sin in their flesh.[2] Children are not accountable for sin until they reach an age of accountability, which is not at a certain number of years. This refers to whenever they reach an awareness that their actions are actually sin against God, and they have an opportunity to choose God or turn Him down.

I have a sin nature; you have one; every person has one. We get it at birth. We become accountable to God as we become aware of our sin.

The Law

God loves His people very much, and He instituted a temporary plan that would suffice for those who loved Him and were choosing Him and His ways—a plan that would enable Him to fellowship with His people again.

You see, when sin came in and man died spiritually, man could no longer have proper fellowship with God. God is a spirit being, and we must fellowship with Him in our spirits.

God is light. Man was full of darkness, so the fellowship, oneness, unity, and the relationship between God and man was broken. The Bible says a breach existed between God and man—a break in their compatibility. You might say a wall came down between them—a wall of sin.

God devised the Law, a system of written rules and regulations that man had to live by if he wanted to be holy enough, right enough, to be God's friend. The Law was perfect and holy, just and good. It stated clearly what man had to do in order to be holy.

Before Adam sinned, he instinctively knew what God wanted and did not want. They were one in Spirit, one in heart, one in purpose. After man sinned, he was no longer sensitive to God. He was hardened by sin and the results of sin. He no longer knew God's heart or ways—they had to be written down.

Man could not do God's will any longer from his heart or out of his spirit. He had to try to please God in his natural ability. But man was unable to keep *all* of the Law perfectly, because man was no longer perfect and never would be again as long as he lived on the earth.

God's Law said if you break the Law in one point, you

are guilty of it all (James 2:10). The Law was perfect, and to keep it all, man needed to be perfect.

Sacrifices

Since man had the Law but could never keep it, no matter how hard he tried, God instituted a system of sacrifices that man could make to atone (make up) for his failures. They were blood sacrifices. The shedding of blood had to be involved. This may sound rather gross, but the reason behind it makes it understandable. When God breathed into Adam the breath of life, he became a living soul, and his blood was filled with life. His blood began to flow through his body. The Bible says, "The life of the flesh is in the blood" (Lev. 17:11). You know this is true. No one lives without blood. If you stop the blood flow, you stop the life.

When Satan tempted Adam and Eve and they chose to sin, sin eventually brought death (Rom. 5:12), and all that death represents: sickness, disease, poverty, war, anger, greed, and jealousy. *The only thing strong enough to cover death is life.*

When man broke the Law and sinned, it was a type of death. The only atonement for sin was blood sacrifice because the life is in the blood (Lev. 17:11).

Another reason God ordained this was to illustrate the good plan He had in mind for man, which He would fulfill in His perfect timing. The prophets were foretelling the coming of a Messiah, a Savior, a Redeemer, One Who would deliver them. God was getting the message out. Remember, if God says it, He eventually does it.

This Messiah would become man's sacrifice, the final sacrifice, a perfect sacrifice. He would be the flawless Lamb of God. No longer would man need to offer lambs without blemish on the altars in the temple as a sacrifice for his sin. Jesus would come, and His sacrifice would put an end to the system of the Law.

Let me quote just one of those prophecies:

He was despised and rejected and forsaken by men, a Man of sorrows and pains, and acquainted with grief and sickness; and like One from Whom men hide their faces He was despised, and we did not appreciate His worth or have any esteem for Him.

Surely He has borne our griefs (sicknesses, weaknesses, and distresses) and carried our sorrows and pains [of punishment], yet we [ignorantly] considered Him stricken, smitten, and afflicted by God [as if with leprosy].

But He was wounded for our transgressions, He was bruised for our guilt and iniquities; the chastisement [needful to obtain] peace and well-being for us was upon Him, and with the stripes [that wounded] Him we are healed and made whole.

All we like sheep have gone astray, we have turned every one to his own way; and the Lord has made to light upon Him the guilt and iniquity of us all.

He was oppressed, [yet when] He was afflicted, He was submissive and opened not His mouth; like a lamb that is led to the slaughter, and as a sheep before her shearers is dumb, so He opened not His mouth. (Isa. 53:3–7 AMP)

The prophecies were being given. People were waiting for their Messiah, their Savior and Deliverer. I do not believe they even truly understood what they were waiting for.

They did not understand that He would deliver them from the Law, from the works involved in trying to please God with perfection when it is impossible. They did not understand that He, Jesus, the Messiah, Savior of the world, would shed His own blood on a cross, let His blood flow, *pouring out His life to remove all sin* from every generation.[3] They were waiting, but they could not understand what was coming.

Jesus Comes

God's time came. The Holy Spirit appeared to a young virgin named Mary. She became pregnant by the miracle-working power of God—pregnant with Jesus, the Son of God. It had to happen this way.

Jesus was already in heaven spiritually and had always been. He was with God from the beginning. But now He was going to take on flesh so He could help the rest of the fleshly humans. They were in a mess from which they had no escape without a Savior.

John 1:1, 14 says that Jesus is the Word of God and that the Word of God became flesh and dwelt among men. Hebrews 4:15 says Jesus is a High Priest who understands our weaknesses and failures because He, having had a fleshly body and a natural soul, "was in all points tempted [just] as we are, *yet without sin.*" Beloved, this is the big difference.

Jesus is alive to God inside, totally connected with the Father. He is one with Him, as Adam was before he sinned. The Bible calls Him "the second Adam" (see 1 Cor. 15:45, 47). Romans 5:12–21 says if one man's (Adam's) sin caused all men to sin, then how much more can one Man's (Jesus') righteousness make all men right with God?

Adam's sinful nature came down on you from generation to generation. Now, *if you will believe it,* the second Adam, Jesus, is waiting to give you His righteousness. Adam was a man, full of God, full of God's life. Sin came and man was filled with darkness. The light in him went out.

Are you full of darkness or light?

Jesus was also a man, born of a woman, but He was full of God. Adam sinned. Jesus did not ever sin; He was the perfect sacrifice for sin.

The Old Testament believers had to constantly make sacrifices for their sins, but the guilt was always there.

Do you feel guilty or free? Dirty or clean?

Jesus became the sinless, sacrificial Lamb of God who took away the sin of the world. Hebrews 10:11–14 says:

Furthermore, every [human] priest stands [at his altar of service] ministering daily, offering the same sacrifices over and over again, which never are able to strip [from every side of us] the sins [that envelop us] and take them away—

*Whereas this One [Christ], after He had offered a
single sacrifice for our sins [that shall avail] for all
time, sat down at the right hand of God,*

*Then to wait until His enemies should be made a stool
beneath His feet.*

*For by a single offering He has forever completely
cleansed and perfected those who are consecrated and
made holy.* (AMP)

The Old Testament priests offered the sacrifices on
behalf of the people. They had to do it over and over, all
the time, always working, trying to be good, always fail-
ing, never feeling good about themselves (inwardly), always trying to *be* good so they could *feel* good.

But Hebrews shows us that Jesus offered Himself once
and for all, the perfect sacrifice. He kept all the law. *His
victory is available to all who will believe.*

4

What Should You Believe?

Believe that Jesus did what the Bible says. Believe He is indeed the Son of God, born of a virgin. He took man's sin on Himself. He became our sacrifice and died on the cross. He did not stay dead. He was in the grave three days. During that time, He entered hell and defeated Satan.

All this He did willingly because He loved His Father (God) and because God and Jesus loved you and me so much that no plan was too extreme. Whatever it took to get God's people back, free again, is what They would do. *Jesus paid* for our sins on the cross. He died and was buried. Then, as God had promised, on the third day Jesus rose from the dead.

What Happened on the Cross

When Jesus hung on the cross, He took our sin upon Himself. God cannot stay in the presence of sin. As Jesus took our sin, He was separated from the fellowship of the Father (Matt. 27:46).

Jesus was taking your sins and those of everyone else upon Him as He felt this absence of His Father's presence. He said, "My God, my God, why have you forsaken me?" (see Matt. 27:46). Jesus knew it would happen, but the horror of separation from the bright presence of the Father was worse than He could have imagined, and it caused Him to cry out. He committed His spirit to the Father and died.

You cannot go to heaven unless you believe with all your heart that Jesus *became your substitute and took all the punishment you deserve. He bore all your sins. He paid the debt you owe.*

He did it for you because He loves you. John 3:16 says:

For God so loved the world, that he gave his only begotten Son, that whosoever believeth in him should not perish, but have everlasting life.

Jesus died for *you*. He paid for *your* sins. God was faithful to Jesus. God did what He told Jesus He would do. He raised Him from the dead.

During the three days His body lay in the tomb, He descended into hell and on the third day, He rose from the dead victorious (Acts 2:27, 31).

What else do you need to believe?

Believe He did it for you.

Believe it with your heart. Your head will not grasp what I am telling you, but believe it with your heart. Listen to your spirit.

Romans 10:9 says that if you confess with your mouth that Jesus is Lord and believe with your heart that God raised Him from the dead, you will be saved.

At this point, if you have decided you believe what I am telling you and you want to receive Jesus, you need to say: "I believe Jesus is the Son of God. I believe He died for me. I believe God raised Him from the dead."

Romans 10:10 says that "with the heart a person believes and . . . so is justified" (AMP). The word "justified" means *made as if he never sinned;* it means cleansed, made right with God. Only believing in Jesus and all He did will justify you.

No amount of good works will ever make you right with God. Merely going to church will not justify you. You must be justified through faith; then good works, such as going to church, will follow as a sign of your heart change. The heart must be right first. You *must* believe with your heart, your inner man.

Romans 10:10 further says to confess with your mouth to "confirm" your salvation (AMP). "Confirm" means "establish."[4] Saying what you believe secures it as yours. It nails it down, so to speak.

Summary

To be born again (John 3:3), or saved, you must believe:

- God is (Gen.1:1; Heb. 11:6).
- Jesus is the Son of God, born of a virgin, born of flesh and blood (Matt. 1:18, 23).
- Jesus is God, one part of the Trinity, one part of the triune Godhead (Col. 2:9; Heb. 1:5–8).
- He came in a fleshly body so He could help man (John 1:1, 14; Luke 4:18–21).
- He took on Himself all your sins and bore them in His own body on the cross (Isa. 53:4–5; 2 Cor. 5:21).
- He died for your sins (Heb. 2:9).
- God raised Him from the dead (Luke 24:1–7; Acts 2:32).
- He is now seated at the right hand of the Father in heaven (Heb. 10:12).

- He is available to every person who will believe (Rom. 10:13; John 1:12).
- He will come to live in your human spirit by the power and presence of the Holy Spirit, making you alive to God (Rom. 8:14–16).

This is what it means to accept
Jesus Christ as your Savior.

If you believe these things, then you can:

- Proceed by admitting that you are a sinner in need of a Savior (Rom. 3:23–24).
- Confess your sins to God (1 John 1:9).
- Have a repentant attitude—be willing to turn from your sin and to live a new life for God (Acts 3:19).[5, 6]

Let's Pray

James 4:2 says you have not because you ask not. *Ask Jesus into your heart; ask Him to forgive your sins.* He will forgive you, and He will come to live in your spirit. Your spirit will come alive to God. Here is a sample prayer you may pray, but I encourage you to pour out your heart to God in your own way.

Father God, I believe Jesus Christ is Your Son, the Savior of the world. I believe He died on the cross for me, and He bore all of my sins. I believe Jesus was resurrected from the dead and is now seated at Your right hand. I need You, Jesus. I receive You by faith. Forgive my sins, save me, come to live inside of me. I want to be born again.

If you have sincerely prayed this prayer:

Congratulations!
You have accepted Jesus Christ as your Savior.
You are a new creature (2 Cor. 5:17).
You now are in right relationship with God (2 Cor. 5:21).

Special note: You do not have to have an emotional experience with God to have accepted Jesus Christ as your Savior. You may or may not experience specific feelings. Many people express a feeling of cleansing or relief—a sense that their burdens have been lifted. I encourage you to remember that the Bible nowhere tells us to base our faith on feelings. Nor do you need to remember a certain time when you received Jesus. But you *must* know in your heart that you have accepted Him as your Savior.

All four of my children have accepted Christ, and two of them could not tell you a time when they first believed. They have grown up always knowing Jesus. I certainly believe this is God's best plan. But, thank God, He also has a special plan for those of us who did not have parents who raised us in the nurture and admonition of the Lord.

5

A New Creature
with a Great Future

The Bible teaches us that when we are born again by accepting Christ as our Savior, we become new creatures. Second Corinthians 5:17 tells us:

> *Therefore if any person is [ingrafted] in Christ (the Messiah) he is a new creation (a new creature altogether); the old [previous moral and spiritual condition] has passed away. Behold, the fresh and new has come!* (AMP)

It is exciting to realize that at the time of the new birth, our old moral and spiritual condition completely passes away, and we have an opportunity for a new beginning. I like to say that we become new spiritual clay. The possibilities for us to have great lives are endless.

We do of course need to cooperate with the Holy Spirit and His plan for us. There is much to learn, but at least our past is buried through Jesus, and we are raised to a new life in Him:

For we are God's [own] handiwork (His workman-ship), recreated in Christ Jesus, [born anew] that we may do those good works which God predestined (planned beforehand) for us [taking paths which He prepared ahead of time], that we should walk in them [living the good life which He prearranged and made ready for us to live]. (Eph. 2:10 AMP)

As God's original creation, we were deceived and marred by the devil, but we are re-created in Christ Jesus. God's plan for us is to do good works, to be His representatives on earth. He had this life planned all along and refused to let Satan destroy us.

God gives us a new heart and a new attitude so we can do good works out of love for Him, not out of mere duty. He wants us to live good lives, and He has prearranged this for us. All we need to do is walk in it by faith.

I encourage you to believe that you can have a wonderful future. Your past is gone and cannot dictate what comes next—if you don't allow it to. Perhaps you did not have a good beginning in life, but beloved, you can have a great finish!

After we have accepted Christ, the very nature of God abides in us, and we begin to do things in a very different way. We learn to think and speak differently. Our goals, attitudes, motives, and actions begin to change. First John 3:9 says:

No one born (begotten) of God [deliberately, knowingly, and habitually] practices sin, for God's nature abides in him [His principle of life, the divine sperm, remains permanently within him]; and he cannot practice sinning because he is born (begotten) of God. (AMP)

This Scripture does not mean that we will never sin or make mistakes. It does mean that because we now have a new nature (God's nature), we cannot habitually, purposely, knowingly continue to sin. We cannot do it because we no longer want to.

Our nature has changed. You might say we have had a heart transplant. God has taken hard, stony hearts out of us and given us hearts sensitive and responsive to His touch (see Ezek. 11:19 AMP).

When we sin, we are convicted of our wrongdoing,

and we want to change. We seek God's forgiveness and ask for His help in living a holy life.

As I have noted, we still sin and make mistakes, and we will do so as long as we live, but we will also experience a desire to change and overcome the areas of weakness in our lives. As we study God's Word, we are changed "from glory to glory" (2 Cor. 3:18). God changes us—His Spirit teaches us the truth and leads us to walk in that truth (see John 16:13).

On the day of our new birth, the Holy Spirit begins a good work in us, and He continues that good work right up until the day of Christ's return (Phil. 1:6). We are becoming more like Jesus in our ways. When we accept Christ, the Lord instantly gives us new hearts and renewed spirits, but we work them out through our lifetimes. Take a look at Philippians 2:12–13:

Work out (cultivate, carry out to the goal, and fully complete) your own salvation with reverence and awe and trembling (self-distrust, with serious caution, tenderness of conscience, watchfulness against temptation, timidly shrinking from whatever might offend God and discredit the name of Christ).

[Not in your own strength] for it is God Who is all the while effectually at work in you [energizing and creat-

ing in you the power and desire], both to will and to work for His good pleasure and satisfaction and delight. (AMP)

Once again, we see from the Scriptures that God begins a good work in us, and we are to work with the Holy Spirit to complete it. We don't do it in our own strength; we trust God, we lean on Him, and we believe that He is at work in us, helping us to live for His good pleasure.

If you have accepted Jesus Christ as your Savior, I encourage you to believe that you are now a new creature. Get up every day and do your best. When you make mistakes, admit them and ask God to forgive you. He is faithful to continuously cleanse you from all sin.

In Philippians 3:12–14, the apostle Paul said that he pressed toward the mark of perfection, but he also said that he had not arrived. He let go of the past and daily strained toward the future. I encourage you to let this be your new attitude.

6

Now That I Have Accepted Christ as My Savior, What Should I Do?

Grow

Now that you have accepted Jesus Christ as your Savior, you need to *grow* as a Christian. You have experienced the new birth, so you are a baby Christian. God's desire is that you grow up and become mature—a full-grown believer who walks in God's ways, knows the Word of God, and understands how to hear the voice of God.

Learn the Word

This cannot happen unless you read and study the Word (the Bible). Your spirit and soul (the inner you) need to be fed and nourished so they will get strong. They also need exercise. Just as your body needs food and exercise to stay strong and healthy, so your spirit and soul also need these.

Ask God to lead you to a good church where you can begin to learn His Word. Start to read the Bible. Many modern translations are available today that make the Bible more easily understood than in the past. I like *The Amplified Bible*; however, many other translations are available. Go to a Christian bookstore and select one. As you begin to read the Bible, ask the Holy Spirit (God's Spirit) to help you understand it.

Exercise

The Word of God (the Bible) is the spiritual food you need. *Spiritual exercise* consists of things like praying, singing praise to God, confessing the Word, thinking about the goodness of God, thinking about the Word, giving and fellowshiping with other Christians.

Pray

As you begin your new life with God, talk to Him. He is *always* with you. You will never be alone again. In His Word, He has said, "I will never leave thee, nor forsake thee" (Heb. 13:5). You do not have to struggle with things as you have in the past. Ask the Lord to help you with everything you do. He is your new Partner in life. The *Holy Spirit* is called "the Helper" in the Bible (John 14:16 AMP).

You may notice that I have been referring to the Father (God), the Son (Jesus), and the Holy Spirit. To make sure I am not confusing you, let me remind you that you now serve *one God,* a triune God, the Trinity, and each of the three Persons of the Godhead has a special relationship to your everyday life.

Pray to the Father in Jesus' name through the power and leading of the Holy Spirit, who is now living inside you, bringing you the presence and reality of the Father and Son.

Water Baptism

You will need to be baptized as soon as possible. Do not put it off any longer than necessary. The Bible teaches that a person should be baptized after he or she accepts Jesus as Lord and Savior.

Baptism means "to submerge in water." Usually a spiritual leader assists you and prays over you as you go down into the water and are brought back up.

This signifies the burial of the old way of living and is an outward sign of you declaring your decision to live for God. Romans 6 teaches us that we are buried with Christ in the waters of baptism and raised to a new life when we come up out of the water.

Again, water baptism is an outward sign that you have made a decision to follow Jesus. He is now your Lord. You are burying your old, sinful ways and are making a commitment to learn new ways of living. The Bible says that through Jesus' death and resurrection, He opened up "a new and living way" (Heb. 10:20).

You must be *committed* to this new way and to these new principles, or the devil will cause you to backslide. First Peter 3:21 says that baptism is a figure of deliverance. It also says you are demonstrating what you believe to be yours in Jesus Christ.

If you were baptized as a baby, which many people are as a religious formality, I suggest you go ahead and be baptized again. Now you understand it and can exercise your faith to believe what the Bible says about baptism.

Formal acts such as baptism mean nothing if there is no real faith involved. Religious works are man's ideas of God's expectations—a formal system of man-made doctrines (some according to God's Word and usually some not) that give rules and regulations we must follow in order to please God. This system does not impart life to the inner man, and it causes people to get into "works of the flesh," trying to please God.

People begin to follow church rules—things that are good in themselves, but if they have no meaning to the participants, they are lifeless. But now that you have a relationship with God through Jesus, you can be baptized, and it will mean something because faith is present.

Learning God's Word, praying, and being baptized are all ways you declare your new faith in Jesus Christ.

7

Is There Anything Else?

Yes! There is one more very important thing you need to know.

There is yet another blessing available to you. The Bible calls it "the baptism of the Holy Spirit." The Bible tells us Jesus baptized people with the Holy Ghost and fire (Matt. 3:4–6, 11).

In Acts 1:8, Jesus talked about this Spirit baptism. He said we would "receive power (ability, efficiency, and might) when the Holy Spirit has come upon you," and this power would cause us to tell others about Jesus (AMP).

When you received Jesus, you received the Holy Spirit into your human spirit. But the baptism of the Spirit is a complete filling. He fills you, and you are placed into Him. It is like asking the Spirit to fill you through and through with the power and ability to live the Christian life and serve God according to His will.

The Greek word *dunamis*, translated "power" in Acts, actually means "miraculous power, ability, might, and strength."[7] Miracle-working power!

Ask yourself: *Do I need power, ability, strength, and miracles in my life?* If you answer yes, then you need to be baptized in the Holy Spirit.

Scriptural References for Being Baptized in the Holy Spirit

- "But you shall receive power (ability, efficiency, and might) when the Holy Spirit has come upon you, and you shall be My witnesses in Jerusalem and all Judea and Samaria and to the ends (the very bounds) of the earth" (Acts 1:8 AMP).
- "And when the day of Pentecost had fully come, they were all assembled together in one place, when suddenly there came a sound from heaven like the rushing of a violent tempest blast, and it filled the whole house in which they were sitting. And there appeared to them tongues resembling fire, which were separated *and* distributed and which settled on each one of them. And they were all filled (diffused throughout their souls) with the Holy Spirit and began to speak in

other (different, foreign) languages (tongues), as the Spirit kept giving them clear *and* loud expression [in each tongue in appropriate words]" (Acts 2:1–4 AMP).

- "Then [the apostles] laid their hands on them one by one, and they received the Holy Spirit" (Acts 8:17 AMP).
- "While Peter was still speaking these words, the Holy Spirit fell on all who were listening to the message. And the believers from among the circumcised [the Jews] who came with Peter were surprised *and* amazed, because the free gift of the Holy Spirit had been bestowed *and* poured out largely even on the Gentiles. For they heard them talking in [unknown] tongues (languages) and extolling *and* magnifying God" (Acts 10:44–46 AMP).
- "And as Paul laid his hands upon them, the Holy Spirit came on them; and they spoke in [foreign, unknown] tongues (languages) and prophesied" (Acts 19:6 AMP).

Tongues

You probably noticed that people began to "speak in tongues" or "other tongues" as they were baptized in the Holy Spirit.

This means a language other than their usual one. It could be a known tongue (to someone else, not the speaker) or a tongue of angels (one unknown to any human) (1 Cor. 13:1). The best and easiest way to describe tongues is to say it is a *spiritual* language, one the Holy Spirit chooses to speak through you but one you do not know. It is the Holy Spirit speaking directly to God through you.

Tongues is referred to as a "phenomenon." That means we do not understand it with our minds. It is a spiritual thing. When you pray in other tongues you are speaking secrets and mysteries unto God (1 Cor. 14:2).

Paul said in 1 Corinthians 14:14 that if you pray in tongues, your mind is unfruitful. In 14:4, Paul says when you pray in tongues, you edify (build up) yourself.

Praying in tongues is one way to be assured that you can pray a perfect prayer when you are in a situation in which you do not know how to pray as you should. Romans 8:26 says,

> So too the [Holy] Spirit comes to our aid and bears us up in our weakness; for we do not know what prayer to offer nor how to offer it worthily as we ought, but the Spirit Himself goes to meet our supplication and pleads in our behalf with unspeakable yearnings and groanings too deep for utterance. (AMP)

Praying in the Spirit, or speaking in tongues, strengthens your spirit. It builds you up spiritually. Jude 1:20 says:

But you, beloved, build yourselves up [founded] on your most holy faith [make progress, rise like an edifice higher and higher], praying in the Holy Spirit. (AMP)

Laying on of Hands

You may receive the Holy Spirit by having someone lay hands on you and pray for you.

By Faith

Luke 11:13 tells us:

If you then, evil as you are, know how to give good gifts [gifts that are to their advantage] to your children, how much more will your heavenly Father give the Holy Spirit to those who ask and *continue to ask Him!* (AMP)

Therefore, ask. You may ask God yourself.

The Holy Spirit May Come Sovereignly

I received the baptism of the Holy Spirit in my car in February 1976 as a sovereign move of God in my life. I was crying out to God, asking for more of Him. I said, "God, there has to be more to Christianity than I am experiencing." I wanted victory over my problems, and I did not have it.

I had received Christ as my Savior many years before receiving the baptism of the Holy Spirit. I was saved and would have gone to heaven had I died. Yet I was without *power* to live a victorious Christian life. I cried out in desperation that morning, and that same evening Jesus baptized me in the Holy Spirit.

I did not speak in tongues right away (mainly because I knew *nothing* about such things). However, I did receive much power, ability, determination, and understanding. During the next three weeks, God led me to radio programs and books where I learned about the baptism in the Spirit.

At first, I did not know what had happened to me. I just knew it was wonderful, and it was of God. I then learned about the gift of speaking in tongues, asked God for it, and received it.

How to Receive Tongues

Ask God to fill you and to baptize you in the Holy Spirit. Simply pray, "Father, in Jesus' name, I ask You to baptize me in the Holy Spirit with the evidence of speaking in tongues."

Be relaxed and at ease in God's presence. He loves you and wants you to have His best. Wait on Him quietly, and believe you are receiving. Believe before you *feel* any change. You *may* feel a change taking place, but you may not. Do not be led by your feelings; be led by God's promises.

To speak in tongues, open your mouth, and as the Spirit gives you utterance, speak forth what you hear coming up out of your inner man. *It will not come out of your head.* Remember, your mind does not understand spiritual things. That is why it is so hard for many people. We are accustomed to our minds running our lives. This whole book is about learning to live spiritually, not naturally.

You will hear or sense syllables, words, phrases, or other utterances that are unusual or foreign sounding to you. Take a step of faith and utter them; speak them forth. Acts 2:4 says, "They . . . began to speak with other tongues, as the Spirit gave them utterance."

You may now use this language (which will grow as you grow and as you exercise the gift) anytime you pray or just to edify yourself. Do not speak in tongues around people who do not understand. Tongues brought forth in a church setting should be interpreted or explained.

Enjoy your new life in the Spirit!

DID YOU MAKE THE RIGHT DECISION?

If you received Jesus or the baptism of the Holy Spirit as a result of reading this book, please call or write and let us know. It will encourage us. We would like to pray for you and rejoice with you.

Smile!
Jesus Loves You!

"Choose for yourselves this day whom you will serve . . . but as for me and my house, we will serve the Lord."

Joshua 24:15 (AMP)

As you begin your new walk with God, it is important that you receive sound spiritual teaching on a regular basis. The Word of God is the spiritual food you need for spiritual growth.

In John 8:31–32, Jesus said, "If you abide in My word . . . you are truly My disciples. And you will know the Truth, and the Truth will set you free" (AMP). I exhort you to take hold of God's Word, plant it deep in your heart, and as you look into the Word, you will be transformed into the image of Jesus Christ (2 Cor. 3:18).

I love you and want you to have God's best. Send in your prayer requests, and we will be happy to pray for you.

With love,
Joyce

Notes

1. The Church is not a building. It is made up of all born-again believers who ever lived.
2. Man's flesh equals his body and soul.
3. Remember that the life is in the blood (see Lev. 17:11).
4. W. E. Vine, *An Expository Dictionary of New Testament Words* (Old Tappan, N.J.: Fleming H. Revell Company, 1940), 226.
5. Special note: If you have ever been involved in the occult in any way, I ask now that you repent of that activity before choosing to accept Jesus Christ as your Savior. Any occult activity is sin and should be repented of along with all other sin. Witchcraft, séances, black or white magic, non-Christian Eastern religions, cults, astrology, and the consulting of fortune-tellers, Ouija boards, mediums, wizards, and psychics are all an abomination to God (see Deut. 18:9–12). I have specifically mentioned these areas because many people today claim to be Christians and yet see nothing wrong with dabbling in or even practicing such biblically condemned activities. Some even participate in these things for "entertainment," not realizing they are placing themselves in great danger.
6. Scriptures regarding accepting Jesus Christ as your Savior: John 3:16; Ephesians 2:8–9; Romans 10:9–10; 1 Corinthians 15:3–4; 1 John 1:9, 4:14–16, 5:1, 12–13.
7. James Strong, "Greek Dictionary of the New Testament," *The Exhaustive Concordance of the Bible* (McLean, Va.: MacDonald Publishing, 1978), 24.

ABOUT THE AUTHOR

JOYCE MEYER has been teaching the Word of God since 1976 and in full-time ministry since 1980. She is the best-selling author of more than seventy inspirational books, including *Approval Addiction*, *In Pursuit of Peace*, *How to Hear from God*, and *Battlefield of the Mind*. She has also released thousands of audio teachings as well as a complete video library. Joyce's *Enjoying Everyday Life®* radio and television programs are broadcast around the world, and she travels extensively conducting conferences. Joyce and her husband, Dave, are the parents of four grown children and make their home in St. Louis, Missouri.

To Contact the Author

Joyce Meyer Ministries
P. O. Box 655
Fenton, Missouri 63026
or call: (636) 349-0303
Internet Address:
www.joycemeyer.org

Your prayer requests are
welcome.

In Canada, please write:
Joyce Meyer Ministries
Canada, Inc.
Lambeth Box 1300
London, ON N6P IT5
or call: (636) 349-0303

In Australia, please write:
Joyce Meyer Ministries
Australia
Locked Bag 77
Mansfield Delivery Centre
Queensland 4122
or call: (07) 3349-1200

In England, please write:
Joyce Meyer Ministries
P. O. Box 1549
Windsor SL4 1GT
or call: (0) 1753-831102

In South Africa, please write:
Joyce Meyer Ministries
P. O. Box 5
Cape Town, 8000
South Africa
or call: (27) 21-701-1056

OTHER BOOKS BY JOYCE MEYER

Battlefield of the Mind *

*Battlefield of the Mind
Devotional*

Approval Addiction

Ending Your Day Right

In Pursuit of Peace

*The Secret Power of Speaking
God's Word*

Seven Things That Steal Your Joy

Starting Your Day Right

Beauty for Ashes Revised Edition

How to Hear from God *

Knowing God Intimately

The Power of Forgiveness

The Power of Determination

The Power of Being Positive

The Secrets of Spiritual Power

The Battle Belongs to the Lord

The Secrets to Exceptional Living

*Eight Ways to Keep the Devil
Under Your Feet*

Teenagers Are People Too!

Filled with the Spirit

Celebration of Simplicity

The Joy of Believing Prayer

Never Lose Heart

*Being the Person God Made
You to Be*

A Leader in the Making

"Good Morning, This Is God!"

*Jesus—Name Above All
Names*

Making Marriage Work
(Previously published as
Help Me—I'm Married!)

Reduce Me to Love

Be Healed in Jesus' Name

*How to Succeed at Being
Yourself*

*Weary Warriors, Fainting
Saints*

Life in the Word Devotional

Be Anxious for Nothing *

Straight Talk Omnibus

Don't Dread

* Study Guide available for this title

JOYCE MEYER SPANISH TITLES

BOOKS BY DAVE MEYER